Panama CANAL
"The Big Ditch"

A PERSONAL HISTORY

To Tom and Andrea, the great musical influences in my life
Josy Mintel

by

Josephine Mintel

Copyright © 2005 by Josephine Mintel.
28231-MINT
Library of Congress Number: 2005901758
ISBN: Softcover 1-4134-8841-2

All rights reserved. No part of this book may
be reproduced or transmitted in any form or by
any means, electronic or mechanical, including
photocopying, recording, or by any information
storage and retrieval system, without permission
in writing from the copyright owner.

This book was printed in the United States
of America.

To order additional copies of this book, contact:
Xlibris Corporation
1-888-795-4274
www.Xlibris.com
Orders@Xlibris.com

Table of Contents

Panama Canal
"The Big Ditch"

Topic	Page Number
Introduction	5
Life in the Zone	7
Panama Railroad	9
The Panama Canal	11
The People of Panama	13
Pirates	14
The San Blas Indians	15
Traditional Panamanian Culture	15
The Panamanian Jungle	17
A Day in the Life	20
More Recent Connections	25
Panama Poetry	27
Panama Vocabulary	29
Bibliography	31

Dedication

This book is dedicated to my Grandpa, otherwise known as "Bud" or Dr. Avery P. King. He has always been the provider for the King family and he is the bravest person I know. I have always looked up to him.

I love you Grandpa. Please let this book serve as a reminder of that love.

Introduction

As a child my Mom grew up in Panama near the Canal. Her Father (my Grandfather) was in the Army and that's why my Mom's family lived in Panama. In this book, I will share my mother's experiences as a "military brat" in Panama and how the Canal affected her life and the life of her family.

Dr. Avery P. King (my grandfather) was a Lieutenant Colonel in the Army. In 1953 when my Mom was 5 years old, he received orders to move to Panama with his family. This was because the hospital in Panama (**Gorgas** Hospital) needed a surgeon. He took his wife, Agnes (my Gran) and his four children; Jim, Judy (my Mom) Su Christine (Su hated people calling her "Sue") and Andy (the baby of the family).

Dr. Avery Parsons King, Lieutenant Colonel, United States Army; stationed in Panama Canal Zone 1953 to 1957. (My Grandfather).

The King Family in Panama 1954; My Mom, Judy, Granny King (My Great Grandmother), Uncle Andy, Aunt Su and Uncle Jim.

Panama Canal: "The Big Ditch"

The Panama Canal was a part of everyday life for my Family." Says Judy, or Mom to me. "The Army provided a home for our family in a big wooden house on top of **Ancon** Hill. This is near the Pacific end of the Canal and it overlooks Panama City and the Southern mouth of the Canal."

The King family home on Ancon Hill.

The United States Army was in charge of the Panama Canal during the 1950's (The U.S. returned the Canal to Panama by **treaty** in 1999, but the Panamanians needed help to keep it operating smoothly. So now, the Chinese have been hired to control the Canal and run it today.) Grandpa provided medical care to the soldiers who were injured during their stay in Panama. The majority of his work though, was the care of soldiers and other military people who got sick while they were in Panama.

Gorgas Hospital in 1953.

Life in the Zone

The title of this section refers to "The Panama **Canal Zone**" which is the land that the Panamanians gave to the United States by treaty to build and run the Canal. The U. S. was in control of the Panama Canal from 1904 to 1999. During this time the Panama **Canal Zone** was not a part of Panama because the United States controlled it. The Zone was a military base. Therefore, most residents were American. The mainstream language was English, not Spanish as in other parts of Panama. Practically everyone wore American clothing and/or military uniforms.

People shopped for food and American products in a **commissary**. In a foreign country you cannot find the kind of product and luxuries that we have in America. To get them in a place like Panama you go to a **commissary**, which is a shopping area for military families People also bought things off of boats passing through the Canal or they went to the Panamanian sector to shop.

The Commissary

"When I lived in Panama," my Mom recalls, "our maid, Madeline bought a **koala** bear from people on a boat that was going through the locks. She gave it to me as a pet. Every month we'd go down to the Canal and wait for the Australian boat that had **eucalyptus** leaves and we'd buy some for the **koala** to eat. We had him for about a year."

Panama Canal: "The Big Ditch"

Madeline was a part of my Mom's family when they lived in Panama. Madeline's family was from the West Indies and they originally came from Africa. She lived on the ground floor of my Mom's house between the stilts (which was " . . . . the maid's quarters, the laundry room and such."). She took care of all the children.

This is an example of how the Panama Canal connects the world. My Mom is American and lived in Panama. She had an Australian animal for a pet and an African woman from the West Indies for a Nanny. The **Canal Zone** was a place for all sorts of people from all sorts of places and it remains that way today.

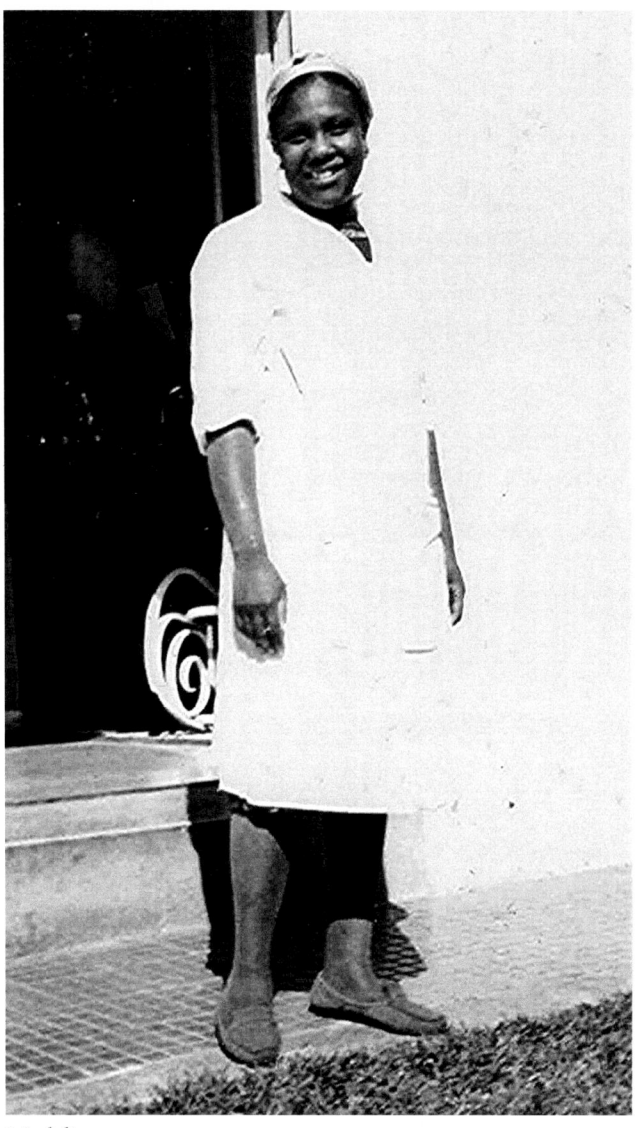

Madeline

The Panama Railroad

Panama Railroad-Train Number 299 (This is the train my mother rode with Madeline and the other children.)

The Panama Railroad was the inspiration for the Panama Canal. In the mid-nineteenth century or around 1850, there was no canal, but there were the beginnings of a railroad.

During the California Gold Rush, people on the East Coast of the United States had two choices on how to get to California: 1. Walk or ride on horseback or in a covered wagon across the entire country, or 2. Ride a boat to the Atlantic side of Panama, go across the Isthmus and then ride another boat from the Pacific side of Panama to San Francisco or elsewhere in California. Most people who could afford it chose the second option. Once they got to Panama these people had another choice. They could 1. Walk 40 miles across Panama through the jungle, or 2. Ride the unfinished railroad as far as it went and walk the rest of the way. Again, most people to chose the second option.

This is the way the Panama Railroad was built. Americans desperate to make their fortune in California paid $10 or more (an outrageous price back then) to ride part way across Panama. The railroad financed itself with the fares people paid. So the railroad was finally finished.

In the late 19th Century or around 1890, most of the United States mail that went from the East Coast to the West Coast and visa versa went through Panama. It had to be carried on the railroad because there was no canal and this is another reason why the railroad was finished.

"When we lived in Panama, Madeline would occasionally take us for a ride on the train on the weekends," Mom remembers. We would bring a picnic lunch and all the kids in the neighborhood would go. It was great fun. We would ride halfway and then get off and catch the second train going back."

Historically, when people believed it was too much trouble to get on a boat in New York or Virginia, off a boat in Panama, onto a train and then hop another boat again . . . then the Panama Canal came into play. With it, a boat from New York could pass all the way through to California making the Panama Canal the most famous shipping canal in the world.

The Panama Canal

The Panama Canal is about 51 miles long. It runs north (from the Atlantic side) to south where it meets the Pacific Ocean across the **Isthmus** of Panama. It is located between North America and South America where the land is the narrowest. The Canal is east of Florida and just a little north of the equator.

While the Panama Canal runs from sea level to sea level, boats going through the Canal have to be lifted over hills that, at one time, were approximately 272 feet above sea level (near the **Gaillard** or **Culebra** Cut). This is done with **locks**. Before the Canal was built, people thought that the Pacific Ocean was higher than the Atlantic Ocean but that proved to be untrue. Sea level is sea level. The difference is in the ocean **tides**. On the Pacific side, the high **tides** are tremendous . . . . 18 to 20 feet high. But on the Atlantic side the high **tides** are barely more than a foot high.

Gatun Locks

Panama Canal: "The Big Ditch"

The Panama Canal has three sets of **locks**. They are called Pedro Miguel and Miraflores locks on the Pacific Ocean side and the Gatun locks on the Atlantic Ocean side. A boat enters the locks being pulled by mules. Mules are motorized vehicles on both sides of the canal that pull the ships through the Canal using large cables tied to the bow of the ship. Once the ship enters a lock, the gates close and the water is allowed to rush in from above, lifting the boat to the next level. The Panama Canal does not use water pumps. Instead, the large amount of rainfall from the tropical climate is collected in Gatun Lake and used to lift the boats. To go down, the ship is enclosed in a lock and the water is allowed to rush out into the ocean.

The People of Panama

"Panama was a very segregated society when I lived there," says my Mom.
The color divide was not black and white, however. Instead, it was gold and silver. This was an historical division based on the way workers on the Panama Canal were paid. During the work building the Canal, there were two separate payrolls: one was skilled, white and American. These workers were paid in gold coins (because America was still on the Gold Standard). The other was unskilled, minority and non-American. These workers were paid in silver balboas, the coins of Panama. On payday, there were two separate lines for being paid: the "gold" line and the "silver" line. This distinction remained when my Mom lived there, but Panama had all kinds of people that didn't fall easily into any categories.

Panamanian Street Scene, 1955

Pirates:

Pirates were a regular feature of Panama's early history. When my Mom lived in Panama in the 1950's, there was evidence of this history. For example, one of her favorite places to play "pirates" with the other military children was at the ruins of Fort San Lorenzo near the Atlantic side of the Canal. Fort San Lorenzo was originally built by the Spanish to protect the riches being discovered in the New World. Pirates would arrive in Panama to steal the pearls, gold and slaves that the Spanish collected to ship back to Spain. Fort San Lorenzo was destroyed and rebuilt several times in several wars and battles over the centuries. It was a wonderful playground for my Mom and her friends.

Panama Pirates. My Gran is in the seated group of Pirates, second from the right with a white blouse and a dagger in her belt. Grandpa is seated in the center wearing a black vest and necklaces.

The San Blas Indians

The Kuna Indians of Panama live in a region within the country of Panama. This region consists of more than 365 islands and a strip of land on the Atlantic coast of Panama. The Kuna people are native people who did not come from Europe. They have been leaders in Indian rights and preservation of natural resources. They have established a large forest preserve on their lands.

Kuna women are known for their colorful costumes which include gold nose rings and the beautifully sewn mola panel blouse. The mola panels of the blouse are hand-woven using several layers of differently colored cotton. The mola may also be decorated with very fine embroidery. Mola panels have become much sought after and collected examples of textile folk art. They are artwork inspired by many different things such as political posters, pictures from books and modern technology as well as themes from traditional Kuna legends. Kuna women spend hours sewing each panel. When they tire of wearing a particular panel, they take it off the blouse and sell it to collectors. The most valuable molas are the ones that have actually been worn as part of a Kuna woman's costume.

My Mom and her family visited several of the San Blas Islands when they lived in Panama. During their visit, Gran bought a mola worn by a Kuna woman. We still have that Mola Panel in a frame hanging in our house today.

Traditional Panamanian Culture

Most Panamanians are descendants of Spanish Conquistadors and other European explorers. One traditional Panamanian costume is called a "Pollera." Yards of white lace with brightly colored and intricate designs sweep across the floor as Panamanian women dance the "tamborito" in their **Polleras**. This luxurious dress consists of ruffles attached to the shawl, off-the-shoulder blouse and a very wide skirt. The dress is made of lightweight linen like a handkerchief. It is heavily decorated with cross-stitch and embroidery, usually in one bright color. This is enough to mesmerize anyone. But there is more. Many gold necklaces are worn and sparkling hair designs are created with gold combs and "tembleques." These headdresses are beads wired in the shape of flowers and bound to hairpins in sets of two worn over

Panama Canal: "The Big Ditch"

each ear. They bounce and tremble as the women move. The men wear shirts embroidered with colorful designs, short pants and the "Ocueño Hat." This means that Carnival and fun are on the way.

Pollera and Carnival in Old Panama

The Panamanian Jungle

Panama is only at 10 degrees latitude. This means it is extremely close to the equator, which explains its tropical climate. This also explains Panama's lush rain forests. The tropical climate of Panama has some negatives and some positives. First, some of the buildings in Panama have iron roofs (at least they did when my Mom lived there) and since the climate was so humid, the roofs would turn bright orange from rust. This was very colorful.

Panama City, 1953

Also, you could never keep your clothes dry if you lived in Panama.

"I remember," says my Mom, "That my mother (Gran) used to try continually to dry our clothes, but whenever we put them back on and went outside our clothes would get soaked immediately from the humidity and stick to our skin." My Mom says she remembers she did not like to wear very much due to this.

Books would grow mold overnight and everything was constantly hot and wet. Madeline lived under the house, which was on stilts, and when it rained really hard, which was often, Madeline would sleep upstairs in my Mom's bedroom while the water ran under the family house down Ancon Hill.

The back of the King Family Home on Ancon Hill showing stilts and wide eaves.

When the Panama railroad and Canal were being built, the wet season was really wet causing conditions that resulted in the birth of many mosquitoes. This resulted in epidemics of **Yellow Fever** and malaria killing many people. This is the bad part.

The good part about all the rain is that the Panama Canal does not need to have water pumps, but can operate using the rainfall to lift the boats through the Canal. It is also good for all the plants and animals that live in Panama.

Judy King, My Mom in Panama 1956

A Day in the Life of My Young Mother

The typical day of my Mom when she lived in Panama would go something like this: Bud (her Dad, my Grandpa) would wake her up in the morning. She'd wash up, get dressed and then Bud would check her shoes for deadly (eeek!) scorpions. There were lots of scorpions in Panama and my Mom is still afraid of them, even now.

After breakfast, my Mom would walk Bud to work. They would both walk together on a cement pathway through the Panamanian jungle down **Ancon** Hill to **Gorgas** Hospital. On the way down there would be few animals on view, but on the way back home when my Mom was alone, she would see numerous animals. There would be sloths hanging from trees. Large iguanas and Gila monsters would waddle across the path in front of her and anteaters would be hunting for food with their snouts in the soft black dirt. Once there was a deer with a small fawn standing near the path. Birds were so numerous and so loud that she sometimes had to hold her ears.

Judy King, My Mom in Panama, 1953

Usually in the tropics you would expect lots of flying bugs, but there weren't many at all in Panama during the 1950's. It was very rare to see a mosquito (yea!). The memory of all that died building the Canal was still fresh in everybody's mind. The bugs were eradicated after so many people died from mosquito born illnesses like **yellow fever** and malaria. My Mom remembers that several times every week a large truck would drive up and down Ancon Hill spraying huge clouds of DDT out the back.

Gorgas Hospital where Bud worked was located on the side of **Ancon** Hill. It was very elaborate with more than 70 buildings and state-of-the-art medial equipment and supplies. At the time, it was said to be one of the best hospitals in the world. Many people thought it was better than any hospital in the United States. It was originally built by the French and then updated by the Americans to help stop all the deaths of workers building and working on the Canal.

Front Entrance to Gorgas Hospital

Once my Mom returned to her house she had to climb about 40 cement stairs to get up to the main part of the house (since it was on stilts). There was a big wide screen that went around most of the house and large eaves extending out from the roof to deal with all the rain. After lunch Mom would ride a yellow school bus to her all-white school. There she learned how to read and she met other military children from America.

Ancon School

After school, my Mom usually went to the beach with Madeline and other children or she went to **Balboa** Yacht Club with Bud to sail his boat ("The Riptide") and have dinner with her family.

My family sailing near Balboa Yacht Club in the "Riptide."

In Panama during the early 1950's, there was no TV. So, in the evenings all the children would gather around the radio to listen to stories and the news. Mom's favorite radio program was "The Lone Ranger."

Each night before bed, Bud would check all the kids' beds for scorpions. Once they got the okay, all the kids including my Mom, would climb under the sheets and go to sleep.

More Recent Panama Connections

My Gran, Agnes, was Howard Baker's campaign manager when he ran for the United States Senate from Tennessee in 1972 and 1978. He won both times. At that time Gran and Grandpa were living in Oak Ridge Tennessee. Howard Baker negotiated the treaty signed in 1977 to return the Canal Zone to Panama before 2000. This is another family connection to Panama and the Canal Zone.

Since my Mom's family left Panama, some have returned by taking cruises through the Canal. The Panamanian people were very hostile to Americans at that time so it was very difficult to visit the places where the family worked, lived and played.

Agnes and Bud King 1956

Panama Canal: "The Big Ditch"

Panama City in 2005

Panama Poetry

The Marmosets: This poem is about my Mom's family and her friends. Jean Bailey, the author, was a next door neighbor of my Mom's family. There are lots of wild animals in Panama including marmosets.

The Marmosets

The marmosets are coming.
They are jumping from limb to limb.
Steve must go and get Judy and Judy will go and get Jim.
Jim will hurry up Su Christine and Andy will follow her fast.
Baby Pat will crow in her pen as everyone pit-a-pats past.

All the children will be quite still
Mike and Nicky and Van
Will bring along Alice to stand and watch
With Libby and Carole Anne.

Then suddenly, out between the leaves
A little white face will show
A little brown body will fly through the air
And back in the Jungle he'll go.

Where do they come from and what do they want?
Nobody seems to know.
"They can't be looking for food," says Jim
"The grass is greener below."

But Su Christine seems to understand and says there's no cause for fuss
"It seems to me," says pony-tailed Su
The marmosets come to see us.

    By Jean Bailey (1955)

Yellow Eyes: This poem is about how Chinese people got the Yellow fever when they came to work building the Canal. In fact this disease is a viral infection that was called "yellow fever" because Asian people were most likely to get it. The poem is very descriptive . . . . ew!

Yellow Eyes

"You are going to have the fever, Yellow eyes!
In about ten days from now
Iron bands will clamp your brow;
Your tongue resemble curdled cream,
A rusty streak the center seam;
Your mouth will taste of untold things
With claws and horns and fins and wings;
Your head will weigh a ton or more,
And forty gales within it roar!
In about ten days from now,
Make to health a parting bow;
For you're going to have the fever, Yellow eyes."

By James Stanley Gilbert

Panama Vocabulary

1. Ancon: The first ship to pass through the recently finished Panama Canal in February of 1914 was the S.S. Ancon, a United States military ship. Ancon Hill where my Mother and her family lived was named after this battle ship.

2. Balboa: Vasco Nunez de Balboa is the name of the first European (Spaniard) to see the Pacific Ocean from Panama. Balboa is now the name of the city that is the operating headquarters for the Panama Canal. Until 1999, Balboa was a part of the Canal Zone and was under the direct control of the Unites States Government. Balboa is located near Ancon Hill where my family lived.

3. "The Big Ditch": A nickname for the Panama Canal.

4. Canal Zone: The land given by Panama to the United States in 1904 to build the Canal. The U.S. controlled it until 1999.

5. Commissary: Shopping center in Panama for American-made goods where my Mom's family bought clothes, groceries and other things.

6. Eucalyptus: Australian trees whose leaves are the primary food of the koala bear.

7. Gaillard Cut: First known as the Culebra Cut, it was the place of highest elevation (272 feet above sea level) through which the Panama Canal was dug.

8. Gila monster: A jungle animal that looks like a dinosaur. It is a lizard.

9. Gorgas: William Gorgas was one of the people in charge of building the Canal. He was in charge of medical care for Canal workers. Gorgas Hospital where my Grandfather worked was named after him.

10. Isthmus: A connection or connector. For example, the Isthmus of Panama is the land that connects North and South America.

11. Koala Bear: Small mammal native to Australia related to the kangaroo. It looks like a small bear.

12. Lock: A boatlift. It has dams on both sides that keep water from flowing in or out when closed.

13. Marmoset: Small monkey common to the jungles of Panama.

14. Molas: Artwork made by the women of the San Blas Indians.

15. Mule: Large motorized vehicle that pulls boats through the Canal.

16. Pollera: Traditional Panamanian costume full of lace with a wide skirt.

17. San Blas Islands: A string of islands in the Caribbean near Panama where Indian culture has been preserved.

18. Tides: The rise and fall of seawater. Tides are caused by variations in gravity between the earth and moon.

19. Treaty: Agreement between governments.

20. Yellow fever: Viral disease carried by mosquitoes that killed many men working on building the Panama Canal. Asians seemed more susceptible to getting it than most other races.

Bibliography

Oral Histories By:
Judith King Mintel
Dr. Avery P. King
James Avery King

Reference Books:

Path Between the Seas: The Creation of the Panama Canal, 1870-1914 By David McCullough, Simon & Schuster (1977)

The Panama Canal, An Informal History of its Concept, Building, and Present Status. By Donald Chidsey, New York: Crown Publishers Inc, 1970.

"Living and Working in the Canal Zone" (March 1953) Booklet Prepared by the Personnel Bureau, the Panama Canal Company, Balboa Heights, Canal Zone—In Cooperation with the Other Offices of the Panama Canal Company and the Canal Zone Government

Web site references:

http://www.pancanal.com/eng/index.html
http://www.ared.com/kora/java/pcc/javaani.html
http://www.june29.com/Tyler/nonfiction/pan2.html
http://thorup.com/cuna.html